Living Green

Planting Trees

By Meg Gaertner

level 2 little blue readers

www.littlebluehousebooks.com

Little Blue House is distributed by North Star Editions:
sales@northstareditions.com | 888-417-0195

Produced for Little Blue House by Red Line Editorial.

Photographs ©: Shutterstock Images, cover, 4 (top), 4 (bottom), 7 (top), 7 (bottom), 8, 11, 15, 16–17, 19, 20–21, 22, 24 (top left), 24 (top right), 24 (bottom left), 24 (bottom right); iStockphoto, 12–13

Library of Congress Control Number: 2022901876

ISBN
978-1-64619-596-1 (hardcover)
978-1-64619-623-4 (paperback)
978-1-64619-674-6 (ebook pdf)
978-1-64619-650-0 (hosted ebook)

Printed in the United States of America
Mankato, MN
082022

About the Author

Meg Gaertner enjoys reading, writing, dancing, and being outside. She lives in Minnesota.

Table of Contents

hole

soil
water

Planting a Tree

A girl digs a hole.

She puts a tree in the hole.

She adds soil and water.

The tree is small now.

But it will grow over time.

Many Benefits

Trees give many benefits.
They help people
and animals.
They also help Earth.

Keeping a house cool costs money. It also uses a lot of energy. Trees can help.

Trees give shade from the sun.

They keep houses cool.

shade

Trees protect houses in winter.

They block cold winds.

Many gases are in the air. Some of them can harm Earth.

Trees use one of these gases. Trees remove it from the air.

Trees are home to many animals. Birds live in trees, and many insects do, too.

bird

Helping Earth

Planting trees helps Earth.

You can plant a tree.

You can help Earth.

Glossary

bird

soil

shade

tree

Index